C000175179

The Isles of Scilly and Beyond

Published by Seagull Publications, Seagull Cottage, Hospital Road,
St. Mary's, Isles of Scilly TR21 0LQ   Telephone (01720) 423030

© Mary Ratcliffe 2004

ISBN 0 9548962 0 3

For Emily, Billy, Matthew, Ella and all my family.
May they, and all who come to the Islands, love its beauty and its Creator.

Jon Kersey

Walkabout on pages 16, 17, 32, and 33, offers an opportunity to
make a pilgrimage on St. Mary's.

Lord you have examined me and know me. You know everything I do; from far away you discern my thoughts...... If I flew away beyond the east or lived in the uttermost parts of the west, you would be there to lead me, you would be there to help me.

Psalm 139

The islands are twenty-eight miles from Land's End, give or take a mile or two! Only when you approach by air do you realise how very small they are. Their beauty is breathtaking and visitors return year after year. In the winter there is a population of about two thousand; in summer that figure is trebled by visitors, many of whom give to islanders, not only their welcome trade, but also their precious friendship.

As you read this little book I hope it will open your eyes again to see the Creator's goodness in things great and small. From the majesty of the ocean surrounding us, to the tiny flowers that grow in the heathland, God's hand is visible.

When you return home, please remember us, and in that remembrance, pray for these beautiful islands and give thanks for God's everlasting goodness to us all.

Can anyone measure the ocean by handfuls, or measure the sky by his hands? Can anyone hold the soil of the earth in a cup or weigh the mountains and hills on scales? ....to whom can God be compared? How can you describe what he is like?

Isaiah 40

The curvature of the earth and the vastness of the sea and sky can be seen from the highest point of any island, and we can realise the truth of these words written by Isaiah. Just as we cannot measure the height, depth, and width of the universe, neither can we measure God's love for everything that he has made. God will never stop caring for his people here, and beyond this horizon.

Let the earth produce all kinds of plants ....so the earth produced all kinds of plants and God was pleased with what he saw.

Genesis 1

The Gardens on Tresco were laid out by Augustus Smith, who came to the Islands in 1834 as leaseholder from the Crown. Rare plants were brought from all corners of the world by Scillonian sea captains. Because many of the plants come from the Southern Hemisphere, they flower throughout the autumn and winter. Christians can also grow and flower in any season and in any place!

Agave fountain, Tresco Gardens

Cromwell's Castle, Tresco

The Lord will be there to teach you, and you will not have to search for him anymore. If you wander off the road to the right or to the left, you will hear his voice behind you saying, "Here is the road. Follow it".

Isaiah 30

Labyrinths are ancient structures found throughout the world, even within cathedrals, e.g., Chartres and Ely. The small one pictured here was, reputedly, built by a keeper of St. Agnes Light. Children delight to tread the path to the centre and find, to their amusement, that there is a way out again.

Lord God, when we do not know which way to travel on our journey of life, help us to remember your promise that if we follow your son, Jesus Christ, we shall find peace in the centre of our being.

You are like light for the whole world. A city built on a hill cannot be hidden. No one lights a lamp and puts it under a bowl; instead he puts it on a lamp stand, where it gives light to everyone in the house. In the same way your light must shine before people, so that they will see the good things you do and praise your Father in heaven.

Matthew 5

Lighthouses surround the islands and, together with navigation marks, they provide a necessary help for all who travel by sea. If you want to avoid the islands, or find a passage through the rocks to a safe anchorage, you need good charts, and a clear eye, to see where you are going. St. Agnes Light was the first, built by The Guild of the Holy Trinity, founded in 1514 by Henry V111. The remains of a chapel near the Daymark on Chapel Down, St. Martin's, could have been built on the site of an earlier light chapel. May Christ, the Light of the World, illumine and guide us on all our journeys.

13

Don't worry about anything, but in all your prayers ask God for what you need, always asking him with a thankful heart.

Philippians 4

How difficult it is not to worry! Much better to transfer our energy into prayer; prayer with thanksgiving, for the many blessings that we have seen and also for those trillions of blessings that have been unseen by us. To place our lives and worries into the hands of God is not an easy thing to do. We long to be independent, yet in that independence of thought, we find fear, instead of peace.

Walkabout - a pilgrimage on St. Mary's

Begin at the Roman Catholic Church, Star of the Sea - Stella Maris, which was originally St Mary's Girls School built in 1860 by Augustus Smith. In the quiet garden, through the entrance to the building, is a plaque reminding us that Scilly has long been a place of safety for travellers on the sea. The Ark and the Dove both found shelter here on their journey with pilgrims bound for America; a journey of faith indeed to sail in such a small craft across the mighty ocean. They found courage to travel to a better land because they had companions in Christ, who believed as they did.

In the upstairs chapel, reflect in silence, that we have many brothers and sisters in Christ and that we too can encourage each other on our journey of faith.

Think about Abram's response to God's call. (Genesis 12) A call which challenged him to move, even at a great age, from a place of safety to an unknown land. Are we being challenged to leave that which is familiar and comfortable, for God's purposes to be fulfilled?

Walk up Buzza Hill taking the first path at the top which leads to a burial chamber. This was constructed about the time of Abraham, 2000 BC, and affords a fine view over Hugh Town and across to Samson, Bryher, Tresco, St. Helen's, Tean and St. Martin's.

Think now about the journey taken by Joseph and Mary to Bethlehem. (Luke 2) They had to make this journey, at a most inconvenient time, because the occupying power demanded a census. Remember those who are daily being forced out of their homes by cruel regimes, starvation, or war, and know that the compassion of our Lord urges us to care for them and for all in need.

16

Passing Buzza Tower, a disused windmill, and the Hospital, take a right turn leading past the Health Centre to Peninnis. It is a long walk along the lane and you may choose to stop at Peninnis Mill for the next meditation.

When Jesus was going to the house of Jairus (Mark 5) to heal his daughter, his journey was interrupted by a woman who had been ill for twelve years. He stopped and healed her before continuing his journey. When he arrived he found that the girl had died but to everyone's astonishment, he restored her to life. We are reminded that plans, carefully laid, can be interrupted by someone in need. Time spent in the service of others is never wasted.

Marvel at the rocks on Peninnis before taking the path to Old Town, pausing at the Church.

This remnant of a much older building has a tranquillity which leads naturally into prayer. Prayer can be turned into song.
A hymn which always springs to mind is:

> O worship the Lord in the beauty of holiness;
> Bow down before him, his glory proclaim.

Don't be ashamed to be heard or seen. Remember Zaccheus, the tax collector. (Luke19) He had probably been watching Jesus and his disciples for some time before Jesus called him down from the sycamore tree.

Reflect as Christians that we are always being watched by our neighbours. Are they watching and waiting for an invitation from us, which will result in their meeting Jesus?

continued on page 32

Lift up your tired hands, then, and strengthen your trembling knees! Keep walking on straight paths, so that the lame foot may not be disabled, but instead be healed. Try to be at peace with everyone, and try to live a holy life, because no one will see the Lord without it.

Hebrews 12

This elegant statue by David Wynn, in Tresco Gardens, shows the joy of childhood. It reminds us that we are designed by God to be part of a family - His family. For any family to grow in love there has to be mutual trust and understanding; a giving and receiving of gifts and service one with another. Each one of us is precious in the sight of God, in the home. In the community of believers we need each other.

The Lord says... Remove the chains of oppression and the yoke of injustice, let the oppressed go free. Share your food with the hungry and open your homes to the homeless poor. Give clothes to those who have nothing to wear and do not refuse to help your own relatives. Then my favour will shine on you like the morning sun.

Isaiah 58

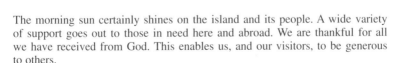

The morning sun certainly shines on the island and its people. A wide variety of support goes out to those in need here and abroad. We are thankful for all we have received from God. This enables us, and our visitors, to be generous to others.

Come to the Lord, the living stone, rejected by man as worthless but chosen by God as valuable. Come as living stones, and let yourselves be used in building the spiritual temple where you will serve as holy priests to offer spiritual and acceptable sacrifices to God through Jesus Christ.

1 Peter 2

Elidius, who lived on the island which we know as St. Helen's, was, according to the Tavistock Abbey records, a bishop and confessor. His feast day is celebrated on 8th August. On the Sunday closest to this day, visitors can make a pilgrimage to the island where a Service is held in the remains of the chapel. It is a special occasion within the church's year when visitors and islanders remember the dedication of St. Elidius who lived and died here in Scilly. After his burial on the island it became a place of pilgrimage for many. A large church was built in the 11th century which was extended in the 12th to accommodate worshippers.

It is humbling, and an inspiration to pilgrims, to remember that Elidius lived simply on this island. Yet through his faithfulness many came to faith. May we too live simply, and be used by God to bring others to a living faith.

Signal Row, St Martin's

Higher Town Bay, St Martin's

And now I make all things new... It is done! I am the first and the last, the beginning and the end. To anyone who is thirsty I will give the right to drink from the spring of the water of life without paying for it. Whoever wins the victory will receive this from me: I will be his God and he will be my son.

Revelation 21

St. Warna's Well is to be found just above St. Warna's Cove on the west of St Agnes, perhaps taking its name from one of the saints who brought Christianity to the islands.
Little is known of these saints, but the fact remains that they came and settled here, often walking and working alongside the inhabitants.

A legend tells us that there was a time when local people would throw pins into the well, in the hope that St. Warna would secure a shipwreck for them. A more pleasing custom, that of throwing a flower into the well, is adopted today. Water is still drawn from wells on all the islands, and is a precious resource, just as is the word of God, when drawn from within the scriptures.

I waited patiently for the Lord's help; He listened to me and heard my cry. He pulled me out of the dangerous pit, out of the dangerous quicksand. He set me safely on a rock and made me secure. He taught me to sing a new song. A song of praise to our God.

Psalm 40

We all have times when our prayers become desperate in their intensity; times when we, or someone we love, is suffering from an illness, or other trouble. We don't know how we, or they, will come through the experience. It is at times like this when we need others to help. God reminds us that there are those, full of his love, who will watch and wait and pray with us. It is up to us to humble ourselves and request their aid. After the pain will come the prayer of thanksgiving.

God's peace, which is far beyond human understanding, will keep your hearts and minds safe in union with Christ Jesus.

Philippians 4

Throughout the year the skies over the islands show the continuing majesty of God's created world. In the midst of stormy weather, shafts of sunlight pierce the cloud.

Life's storms are also pierced when those around us show concern. They are like travelling beams of sunshine showing His love through the clouds of dis-ease.

continued from page 17

In Old Town take the opportunity for refreshment. Perhaps it was when the disciples were resting beside the Jordan at Caesarea Philippi, the most northerly town reached by Jesus, (Mark 8) when they were asked two questions by him; "Who do people say I am?" and "Who do you say I am?"

The disciples pointed out that many recognised Jesus as one of the prophets, like John the Baptist or Elijah, but it was Peter alone who had the courage to declare that Jesus was the Messiah.

The question "Who do you say I am?" is still asked of us.

Is Jesus only a great teacher or is he the Messiah, God's promised Saviour?

Do we have the courage of Peter to declare, "Jesus is Lord," before our friends and companions?

Take the path leading to the Lower Moors Nature Trail.

Rest along the way and recall another journey, this time with Cleopas, on the road to Emmaus, (Luke 24) and another question, "What are you talking about?"

The followers of Jesus spoke of their sadness and disappointment at the events which had happened in Jerusalem. "We had hoped that he would be the one to set Israel free!"

Jesus told them that what had happened had been predicted in the scriptures, that suffering was also necessary before the Messiah could enter into glory.

It was not until they invited Jesus to stay with them, and the subsequent breaking of bread, that they recognised their companion as the Risen Christ. At once they went back to Jerusalem and found to their amazement that he had also appeared to Peter. As they were speaking, the Lord himself stood among them and said "Peace be with you."

Almighty God, help us to understand your word, written by the power of the Holy Spirit, which tells us about the life of Jesus, and brings hope to all who are disappointed and afraid.

32

Taking the path from the pond, and passing through the gardens of the craft workshops, turn left until you come to the steps leading to Harry's walls on Mount Flagon. This is an unfinished fort from which there is a wonderful view of the harbour. It is a good place to finish the walk, especially if you have a picnic!

Before starting your meal remember the day, (John 21) when Jesus was cooking fish on the beach for the disciples, and give thanks for the food, for the beauty of the walk, and for the word of God with its nourishment, inspiration and challenge.

The last journey to recall is the one Paul took to Damascus. (Acts 9) Paul, a Roman citizen brought up as a Hebrew, resented the challenge brought by Jesus. He was determined to have his own way, which was not of God. We need to be thankful to those who challenge the way we see things, in case we are mistaken in our zeal.

Deep peace of the running wave to you.
Deep peace of the flowing air to you.
Deep peace of the quiet earth to you.
Deep peace of the shining stars to you.
Deep peace of the Son of Peace to you.
Today, and always.
　　　　　　　　　Alistair Maclean.

Let lights appear in the sky to separate day from night and to show the time when days, years, and religious festivals begin; they will shine in the sky and give light to the earth - and it was done.

Genesis 1

Everyone likes to look out towards Samson, many wishing to capture the sun as it sets between North and South Hill. Even at sunset the island remains silhouetted against the sky. We have no control over the times of the sun s setting and rising, that was ordained by the Creator. He also created us in his own image, for good! Let us treasure and nurture all that God has created throughout the world.

Come, you that are blessed by my Father! Come and possess the kingdom which has been prepared for you ever since the creation of the world. I was hungry and you fed me, thirsty and you gave me a drink; I was a stranger and you received me in your homes, naked and you clothed me; I was sick and you took care of me, in prison and you visited me.

Matthew 25

One of the joys of a holiday is choosing what to do and where to go. If the weather is good, then in the morning the quay is crowded with holidaymakers who have chosen to go to an off- island, maybe for a stroll on Shipman Head, Bryher, or to Tresco and it s world famous gardens; St. Agnes, and across the bar to Gugh, or St. Martin's and a walk to the Daymark.   Our normal lives are often so ordered that we have little or no choice about what we do, but here our duties are forgotten and we have the freedom to choose how we spend our days. Thank God for the freedom of choice that we can enjoy, and pray for all who have no choice about how to spend their days because of hunger, loneliness, or imprisonment.

He was still a long way from home when his father saw him; his heart was filled with pity, and he ran, threw his arms around his son, and kissed him.

Luke 15

There are many comings and goings on the islands. The first sailing of the Scillonian, in spring, brings a thrill of anticipation. Each day she will bring hundreds of passengers and some will be returning home. Holidaymakers, who often wish that they could settle here are sometimes blessed with that reality!

Shipman Head, Bryher

Hell Bay, Bryher

Very early on Sunday morning the women went to the tomb, carrying the spices they had prepared. They found the stone rolled away from the entrance to the tomb, so they went in; but they did not find the body of the Lord Jesus. They stood there puzzled about this, when suddenly two men in bright shining clothes stood by them. Full of fear, the women bowed down to the ground, as the men said to them, "Why are you looking among the dead for one who is alive? He is not here; he has been raised."

Luke 24

In every burial ground on the islands memorial stones give an insight into the lives of past inhabitants. Many were lost at sea, and children often died from diseases which are now curable. Here, in Old Town, many burials took place in 1875, following the wreck of the Schiller. The compassion shown by the islanders at this time was recognised by the German government and no action against the islands was taken during the first world war.

In the sadness that death brings we remember that, "Jesus wept," as we do. We also remember the hope given to us by the resurrection of Jesus, testified to us by Paul in Chapter 1 of his first letter to the Corinthians.

You will show me the path that leads to life, your presence will fill me with joy for ever.

Psalm 16

After many visits to the islands new delights are still to be found in unexplored places. Holidays offer the opportunity to reset the course of our lives. Sometimes we realise that, to be the people God wants us to be, we need to change the way we live.

45

The world and all that is in it belong to the Lord; the earth and all who live on it are his. He built it on the deep waters beneath the earth and laid its foundations in the ocean depths.

Psalm 24

The seas crash against the shoreline of Peninnis Head, like the sound of thunder. This is a picture taken on a sunny day when it is good to be out and about. In winter when the weather closes in, and the winds are reaching gale force, it is better to stay indoors, shutting out the storm, and yet remaining conscious of those who travel the seas.

Sam Ratcliffe

47

Islands cradled in a sapphire sea
welcome the visitor,
like me
well worn by life,
into its arms,
overflowing with
tranquillity.

Islands of quiet days when
sound is
the gentle swish of seaweed,
washed against the rocks
by the incoming tide.
The seabirds cry;
allowing time
to think again of the Creator's
goodness
in ordering all things,
and remembering,
as the tide sweeps over the troubled
sand,
His covering grace over those who
love Him.

Ringed plovers,
marathon runners,
hastily gathering
food on their journey,
search crevices for treasure.

May we, summer migrants too,
stay and search,
for riches.

Soon days of peace
will be a treasure store
to draw upon and give to others,
jewels from our rest.

Lord,
I thank you for all the joys we've
known
In these Islands of the Blest.

Where shall I gather flowers fair
to lay upon the table for my Lord ?
A special offering, from a grateful heart,
for His sweet love to me?

For sleep
elusive sleep,
has now been given
in abundance.
Sleep, laced with sunshine and birdsong
to replace the tears of night.

The air is still, my heart at peace.

I see that all around us overflows
with given beauty, unordered ,
yet perfect, in harmony with sea and
sky.
Fair fennel, sweetening the air.
Vines of convolvulus climbing upwards
to the sun,
the bramble flowers grey,
soon to be filled with hue of blood.
The rain-dropped thorns;
These given for my use.

The sky
above the tiny island church
was Agapanthus blue.
Inside all was at peace.

Upon the font and altar,
flowers breathed new life
fresh from the sun and wind.
The golden gifts along the path
providing a most worthy offering -
for the King of Kings.

To those who win the victory I will give some of the hidden manna. I will also give each of them a white stone on which is written a new name that no one knows except the one who receives it.

Revelation 2

Little remains of the abbey on Tresco. Like much of the island's history, there is no certain evidence pointing to the exact time of it's foundation or dissolution. These arches, and a few gravestones, are all that remain of the 13th century building. A great amount of the material from the Abbey was used in the construction of the new gardens by Augustus Smith. Two monuments, one on Tresco and one on St. Mary's, show how important he was to these islands. A memorial stone beneath the smallest of the arches is the oldest Christian artefact in Scilly. The inscription reads THI FILI .... COGI, and it is believed to date from AD550.

Sam Ratcliffe

What we see now is like a dim image in a mirror; then we shall see face to face. What I know now is only partial; then it will be complete - as complete as God's knowledge of me. Meanwhile these three remain: faith, hope, and love; and the greatest of these is love.

1 Corinthians 13

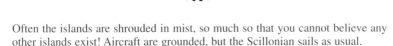

Often the islands are shrouded in mist, so much so that you cannot believe any other islands exist! Aircraft are grounded, but the Scillonian sails as usual.

Though the dawn breaks cheerless on this isle today,
my spirit walks upon a path of light.
For I know my greatness.
Thou hast built me a throne within Thy heart.
I dwell safely within the circle of Thy care.
I cannot for a moment fall out of the everlasting arms.
I am on my way to Thy glory.

Alistair Maclean.

And why worry about clothes? Look how the wild flowers grow: they do not work or make clothes for themselves. But I tell you that not even Solomon in all his wealth had clothes as beautiful as one of these flowers.................so do not worry about tomorrow.

Matthew 6

Wild flowers grow in abundance on the islands. Many species which do not grow on the mainland thrive here. Flowers or plants which were originally introduced as crops or even as garden plants, are also to be found. Many succulents from exotic parts of the world grow on our shores, notably the dew plants, mesembryanthemums and rhodostachys. Bermuda buttercup, (which incidentally is not from Bermuda, nor is it a buttercup, but an oxalis), together with corn marigolds, cover the bulb fields in a golden hue throughout the summer.

Sandbar. St Agnes - Gugh.

Peninnis.

The Kingdom of heaven is like this. A man happens to find a treasure hidden in a field. He covers it up again, and is so happy that he goes and sells everything he has, and then goes back and buys that field.

Matthew 13

Archaeological treasures are constantly being discovered throughout the islands, and   under the sea. These finds often date from the Bronze Age. Children of all ages love beachcombing. Treasures are always to be discovered in the most unlikely places, but the greatest treasure of all is the discovery that leads to the Kingdom of God.

Then the Lord told Moses to make a metal snake and put it on a pole, so that anyone who was bitten could look at it and be healed.

Numbers 21

The caduceus on the roof of the Health Centre is a universal symbol used by the medical profession. Though it was the symbolic staff of Mercury, others recall that Moses had a rod which had healing properties.

The Health Centre provides our resident doctors and other health professionals with a splendid base to serve the whole community. The medical sea ambulance, takes doctors and nurses to patients on the off islands, and brings patients to St. Mary's Hospital for urgent treatment. If specialist care is needed, then the air ambulance can be used.

"Listen! I stand at the door and knock; if anyone hears my voice and opens the door, I will come into his house and eat with him, and he will eat with me".

Revelation 3

The sturdy doors leading to the Hugh are never closed, just folded back to the wall, reminding us of the time when Star Castle was a military headquarters. The exterior of the Castle and the walls surrounding the Hugh are little changed over the years, but access is easier. So it is with the scriptures. New translations make it easier for us to read, though the transference of knowledge from head to heart can still only be found with God's grace, following a deep desire for understanding. Whilst much of the writings in the book of Revelation remain a mystery, the invitation in this passage has been accepted by many and helped others to understand that Christ does indeed come to anyone who asks him to do so.

May the Lord bless you and take care of you; may the Lord be kind and gracious to you, may the Lord look down on you with favour and give you peace, now and for evermore.

All praise and thanks to God, the Father, now be given,
the Son and Him who reigns with them in highest heaven,
the one eternal God, whom earth and heaven adore,
for thus it was, is now, and shall be evermore.

M. Rinkart